A Simple Guide

to

Skype™

D1515798

by
Rick Winter

LUMINIS BOOKS
Published by Luminis Books
1950 East Greyhound Pass, #18, PMB 280
Carmel, Indiana, 46033, U.S.A.
Copyright © Luminis Books, 2012

PUBLISHER'S NOTICE

Cover art direction and design by Luminis Books. Cover photo courtesy of Shutterstock.

ISBN-10: 1-935462-68-7
ISBN-13: 978-1-935462-68-2
Printed in the United States of America

10 9 8 7 6 5 4 3 2 1

Simple Guides

give you

Just the Facts

Get up to speed with Skype—fast!

Simple Guides: get you started quickly.

No extra clutter, no extra reading.

Learn how to **set up Skype,** as well as how to add and **set up all your friends, family, and other contacts.**

Find out about all the features of Skype, how to **change views, set your status and conduct video and audio only calls.**

Learn about all the different things you can do to **contact your friends and family on Skype for free, and start having fun!**

To Karen, my wonderful wife of 23+13 years.

Acknowledgments

A big thank you to Debbie Abshier of Abshier House for recommending me for this book. Thanks to Chris Katsaropoulos for his insight in establishing the *Simple Guide* series and for handling all the publishing angles such as production and distribution. I'm so glad I reconnected with you. Thanks also to Chris Pichereau for her accurate copy editing.

About the Author

Rick Winter is a mission-driven children's and adult educator with a passion for educational reform. He possesses more than 15 years of school leadership, program management, curriculum design, business development, and writing achievements. He is the author of more than 50 books. For more information, see his web site at www.RickWinter.com.

Table of Contents

Chapter 1

Setting up Skype

Skype was created by Niklas Zennström and Janus Friis in 2003 and was sold to eBay for $2.6 billion dollars in 2005 and then to Microsoft in 2011 for $8.5 billion. The number of accounts is over five hundred million and growing. What's all the fuss?

Skype can act as a communication hub for you and is obviously becoming a communication platform for millions of people. You can use Skype to coordinate your phone calls, contacts, as well as add video and group calls to your communication mix. Skype allows you to collaborate on documents and projects by sharing your screen or sending files to people you are working with.

In order to use Skype you need the following:

- ➢ Windows 2000, XP, Vista, 7, Mobile, Mac OS, iOS, LINUX, or other operating systems.
- ➢ A computer, tablet, or one of more than 50 mobile phones.
- ➢ Built-in speakers or external speaker.
- ➢ A built-in or external microphone
- ➢ A web camera (not required, unless you want your contacts to see you).

This user guide focuses on using Skype from a Windows based computer, however you can use this guide to find out about many of the Skype features.

To Get Started

There are three things you need to do to get started with Skype:

1. Set up a Skype account.
2. Download Skype.
3. Launch Skype from your computer.

Set up Account

To set up an account with Skype:

1. Go to www.Skype.com.

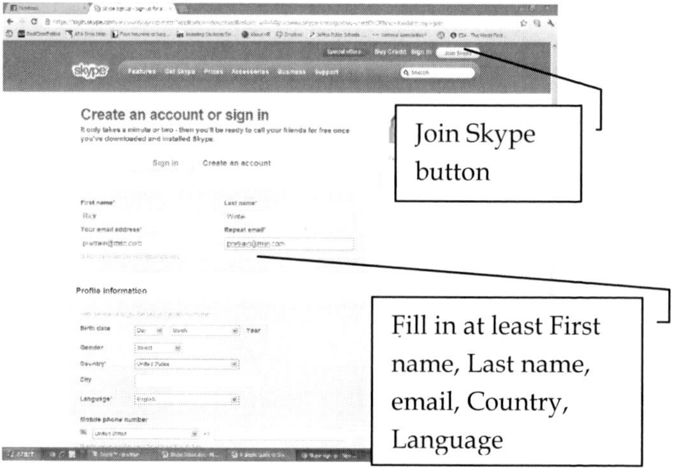

Figure 1-1: Creating a Skype Account.

2. Click the **Join Skype** button.

3. Fill in the requested information – include at minimum, the items marked with an asterisk (**First name**, **Last name**, **Your email address** twice, **Country**, and **Language**).

    a. Fill in your **City** if you have a common name and you want to make it easier for contacts to locate you.

    b. If you include your **Mobile phone number**, this will be visible to your contacts and they can call you from Skype if they have purchased that service.

4. Scroll to the bottom of the form and fill in your **Skype Name**, do not include spaces and include 6-32 characters and/or numbers.

    c. If you type in a name used by someone else, Skype informs you that the name is not available.

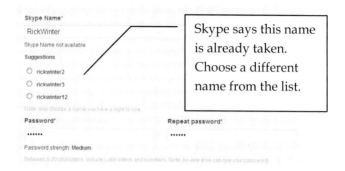

Figure 1-2: Skype suggests usernames.

> d. Skype provides you some suggestions based on your first and last name or you can try other letter/number combinations.

5. Type a **Password** (6-20 characters and/or numbers) and **Repeat password** again for confirmation.

6. Enter security words in the box. This lets Skype know you are a real person and not a computer hacking into the program.

> e. If you cannot read the words, try your best interpretation, click the **Refresh** button, or try the **Listen** button and type the words said between the sounds.

7. Read the Skype Terms of Use and Skype Privacy Statement and click the **I agree – Continue** button.

8.   If you've entered all the required information correctly, Skype sends you to a web page thanking you for registering and giving you offers. Otherwise, Skype displays, "Please review the information that you have entered." Scroll through the form and make corrections as needed.

Install Skype Software

To install the Skype software on your computer:

1.   Go to www.skype.com.

2.   Click **Skype for Windows** or type in **Download** in the **Search** text box and press **Enter**.

3.   Click the **Download Skype** button. If your browser blocks the install, click on the message at the top of the screen, "click **Here for options**" and choose **Download File**.

4.   The File Download – Security Warning dialog box opens. Click **Run**. You may have more than one file to run, so click **Run** again if requested.

5.   The Installing Skype window opens. Read the Skype's Terms of Use and Skype's Privacy Policy, select your language and click **I agree – next**.

6. The next screen asks you to install the Bing Bar. If you already have a search toolbar, you may not want an extra toolbar. If desired, keep the box checked. Otherwise, uncheck the box and click **Continue**.

7. You will see a progress bar for a few minutes. When Skype is done installing, the Thanks for choosing Skype window displays and the Skype software may open in another window.

To Launch Skype

To open Skype, do one of the following:

➤ Double-click on the **Skype desktop icon.**
➤ Double-click the **Skype tray icon.**
➤ Or click the **Start** button, choose **All Programs, Skype, Skype**.

To Launch Skype Automatically

Skype often launches messages when you are using your computer. To avoid these constant messages, you should set up Skype to launch when you start Windows. If you are low on memory, this might not be the best option.

To set up Skype to open automatically when Windows is started:

1. In the Skype window, select **Tools, Options**.

2. If not currently selected, click the **General Settings** bar on the left of the dialog box.

3. Click the **Start Skype when I start Windows** checkbox to add a checkmark (or remove the checkmark to use one of the steps above to launch Skype each time you want to go into the program).

4. Click the **Save** button.

Buy Skype Credit

[$] Like many Internet companies, Skype is attempting to monetize their site. Their strategy includes having a mix of free and paid services. You need to buy Skype credit or get a subscription for many of the services, such as SMS messaging and video conferencing with multiple people. If you're travelling and don't have cheaper options, you might want to buy Skype credit so you can at least attach to a Skype Wi-Fi to get on to your computer. When you see this icon [$] displayed this indicates the Skype service is not free. Of course, Skype may change what may no longer be free at any time. Make sure you review your Skype credit often to see what Skype is doing with your credit.

To buy Skype Credit:

1. Select **Skype, Buy Skype Credit**. After a few moments, the Skype Buy credit dialog box appears.

Figure 1-3: The Buy Credit window allows you to purchase additional credit.

2. If you do not want to automatically have Skype recharge you, uncheck the **Recharge my account** check box.

3. If you want to change the payment method from the last time you paid or signed up, click the **Paying with Change** button.

4. If you want to change your billing address, click the **Billing Address Change** button.

5. When you are ready to make the purchase, click the Buy Now button. The Buy credit dialog box changes to say

that Skype is processing your order.

Figure 1-4: The order number shows in the Buy Skype Credit window. Write down your order number in case you need to refer to it at a later date.

6.   Click the **Close** button to exit the dialog box.

See Your Profile

When you are using Skype, you may want to customize your on screen appearance. You can add a picture to display when people search for you or see an incoming call from you. You can also add your phone numbers and emails, and add a short description about yourself.

To see what your profile looks like to other people:

1. Select **View, Profile**. Your profile displays with all of your current settings.

2. To see what your profile looks like to non-contacts, click the Public profile button.

Figure 1-5: The Public profile shows your picture and other settings that all users can see.

3. To see what your profile looks like to contacts, click the **Contacts only** button.

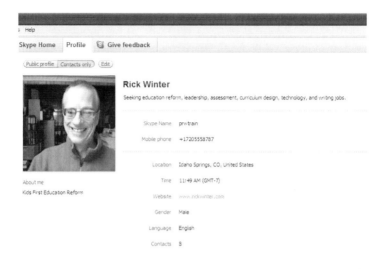

Figure 1-6: Skype shows additional information to your contacts such as your phone number and website.

Change Profile

To change your profile settings:

1. Select **View, Profile** Your profile displays with all of your current settings.

2. To change your profile settings, click the **Edit** button.

Figure 1-7: The Edit Profile screen allows you to make changes directly in the window.

3. Click on the item you want to change. If there is an existing entry, you are taken to a text box. If there is no entry, you can click on the link such as **Add number**. The right part of the screen shows if the information is available to the Public or to your Contacts only.

4. If desired, you can display some information between your contacts or to no one, but only if there is an arrow. Click on the arrow and choose between **Contacts only** or **Private**.

Change Profile Picture

To change your profile picture:

1. Select **View, Profile**. Your profile displays with all of your current settings.

2. Click the Change picture link.

Figure 1-8: Your current picture displays through your web camera.

The Set your picture profile window opens and gives you two options:

    a.   Click **Take a picture** if your web cam is on. You can use the scroll bar to zoom to choose a close up. Click **Use this picture** if you like the one shown better than your existing profile picture.

Figure 1-9: Your current picture from your Web camera displays in the Set your profile picture dialog box.

b. Use the scroll bar to zoom and Use this picture to select the picture shown.

c. Click **Browse**, navigate to the location of a stored picture, and click **Open**.

Watch your Skype Credit

Skype has added some nice features when you are using Skype credit so you can watch your balance and know how much you are spending.

To manage your Skype credit, do any of the following:

➢ To view your balance, open your Skype window. Your current balance appears on the Call phones bar.

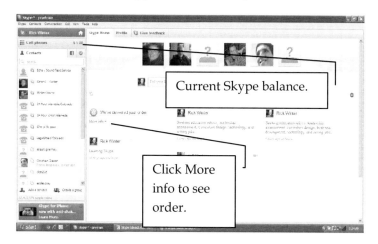

Current Skype balance.

Click More info to see order.

Figure 1-10: Use the Skype Window to check your order status and balance.

➢ If you've recently completed an order, click on the **Skype Home** tab and then click on the **More info** link for your order.

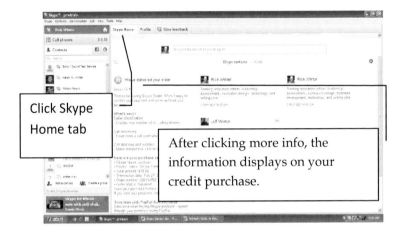

Click Skype Home tab

After clicking more info, the information displays on your credit purchase.

Figure 1-11: Skype allows you to see details about your order.

➢ To see more current details on your account, click the **Call phones** bar with your balance and click the **View account** button. The Account window opens.

Figure 1-12: You can check recent calls and costs for each call.

Get an Online Number

[$] You can pay to obtain an online phone number. When people call you from a phone or a computer, Skype directs the call to any computer you are signed on to with Skype, no matter where you are in the world. There is an additional charge for the online number. Your contacts pay the local fee amount for the phone number.

1. In the Skype window, select **Skype, Account**.

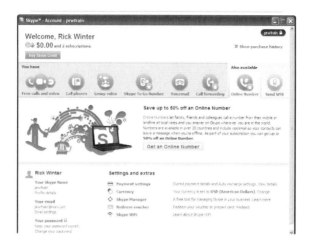

Figure 1-13: Online Number allows friends to call your computer from a landline or mobile phone.

2. Click the **Online Number** icon. The orange asterisk indicates there is an additional charge. If you have another Skype subscription, you may be eligible for a discount. The screen should indicate if you are eligible.

3. Click the **Get an Online Number** button. Your browser launches and list the countries that are available for an online number.

4. Click the flag or your country name.

5. Follow the prompts relevant to your country. For example, in the US Skype asks you to select your state and then prompts you for an area code. Skype will

suggest phone numbers. You can type a phone number in or use a pattern to see if any phone number is available. For example 777* checks for all phone numbers in the area code to see if there are any with three sevens in a row.

6. Click on the phone number to select it.

7. Click the **Continue** button.

8. If you have already entered a credit card or another form of payment, Skype asks you to click the Buy now button to complete the process.

Set up Call Forwarding

[$] Skype can forward your online phone calls to a cell or a landline phone. There is an additional charge for this service. However, if you already have a subscription, there may not be an additional charge.

1. In the Skype window, select **Skype, Account**.

2. Click the **Call Forwarding** icon. The orange asterisk indicates there is an additional charge.

Figure 1-14: Call forwarding allows you to receive Skype calls on your mobile or landline phone if you don't answer the computer call.

3. Select the country from the drop down list and enter the phone number to forward calls to.

4. Click the **Save** button.

Change Call Forwarding Settings

To Disable Call Forwarding or change the settings:

1. In the Skype window, select **Skype, Account**.

2. Click the **Call Forwarding** icon.

3.   If you want to change the phone number, click the **Edit** button and type in a new phone number.

4.   If you want to add a second phone, click **Add another phone number**, select the country and type in the phone number and click **Save**.

5.   If you want to remove call forwarding, click the **Disable** button.

Check for Updates

If it has been awhile since you installed Skype, you should check if there is a newer version to make sure you have all the latest features.

To update Skype:

1.   Select **Help**, **Check for Updates**.

2.   If there are updates available, you will see a dialog box letting you know.

Figure 1-15: The Update box lets you know if you need to update Skype.

3. Click the **Download** button. The dialog box lets you know how much time is remaining. You can **Cancel** the download if you don't have time or **Hide** the dialog box if you want to work on something else.

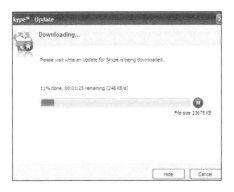

Figure 1-16: After you start the download, the dialog box gives you an estimated time for the download.

4. Once the download is ready to install, the dialog box gives you the opportunity to **Upgrade** or choose **Not now** to do the upgrade later. Click **Upgrade** to make your software current.

Figure 1-17: Choose Upgrade to make the changes now.

5. Skype software may close and you will get a wait screen informing you that Skype is being updated. After Skype is finished, you are returned to the Skype program.

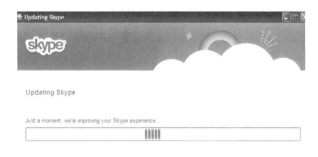

Figure 1-18: This screen indicates that Skype is adding the latest updates.

Premium Subscription

[$] A premium subscription allows you, for a monthly fee, to do things you would not be able to do with the free version of Skype. This includes:

➢ Click to Call (web pages convert phone numbers to buttons you can use to call).

➢ Get voice messaging (you can also pay per call for this with Skype credit).

➢ Call land lines or mobile phones (you can also pay per call for this with Skype credit).

➢ Set up call forwarding.

➢ Get an online phone number.

Set up Premium Subscription

There are multiple ways to set up a premium subscription. In this case we'll assume you are in your Skype window. You could also go to the www.skype.com website.

1. Click on **Skype, Account**. The Account window opens.

Figure 1-19: Skype shows in blue what features you currently have. The Also available section in gray are additional features you can get for a fee or subscription.

2. Click **See subscriptions**. Skype gives you options from for US, Europe, or other plans. Follow the screens to set up your subscription and payment options

Figure 1-20: If you choose United States, Skype gives you options for the US.

3. If you want to change the country, click the **Change country** bar and select a different country.

4. Scroll to the option you wish and click **Buy now**. Complete the screens with the options on how often you want to pay, contact information, and your payment information.

Click to Call

If you have a Premium Subscription, you can click on a phone number on a web page to make a phone call.

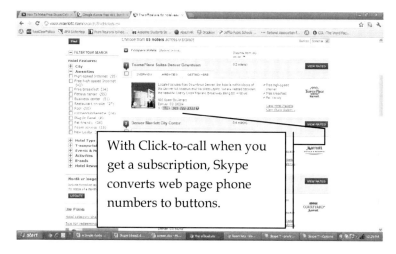

With Click-to-call when you get a subscription, Skype converts web page phone numbers to buttons.

Figure 1-21: Click on a phone number on a web page to make the phone call through Skype.

Chapter 2

Setting up Contacts

Skype allows you to manage your contacts either through the program itself, through Facebook, or through Outlook. You can add individual contacts or import your email list into the program.

Add a Contact

To add a contact:

1. In the Skype window, click on the **Add a contact** button at the bottom of the left pane.

2. The new contact window opens. Type in as much information you know about the contact as possible.

Figure 2-1: You don't have to add all fields for a contact, but the more you do, the better chance you have of finding if the contact is already on Skype.

3. If Skype finds the contact, a picture may appear.

4. Click the **Add** button. One of four things will happen:

    a. The contact appears in your Contacts pane on the left.

    b. Or, if Skype does not find the contact and you have typed an email address, Skype prompts you with an email to invite the person on Skype. You can leave the default email with instructions on how to download Skype and your username or you can type in a different email. Click the Send email button when finished

Figure 2-2: You can send an email to invite a contact.

c. If there are a number of potential matches, Skype gives you an option to choose the contact. Click the **Add contact** button next to the person you want to invite.

d. If Skype finds the person's account, you are given the opportunity to ask the person to add you to Skype (Send request) Or just save the phone number instead.

Figure 2-3: Type a message to the person letting them know who you are.

5. After you add this person, you can click the **Add another contact** button at the bottom of the window or click the **Close** button to return to the Skype window.

Add a Phone Number to a Contact

After you add a contact there are a number of ways you can edit the contact.

To add a phone number to a contact, do the following:

1. Click on the contact name in the left pane.

2. Click the down arrow next to **Call Phone**. A small box
    opens.

**Figure 2-4: In the right pane, choose the Call Phone down
arrow.**

3. Click in the blue **Add phone number** area.

4. If desired, click the first drop-down arrow and choose
    Mobile, Home, Office, or **Other**.

Figure 2-5: You can put in one of four different phone types.

5. If necessary, click the arrow next to the flag and choose the country.

Figure 2-6: Choose your country.

6. Type the new phone number

Figure 2-7: The Add a number to this profile shows your new phone number.

7. Click on the Check button.

Remove a Contact

You can remove of a contact permanently from your contact list.

To remove of a contact:

1. Right click on the contact name in the left pane.

2. Select **Remove from Contacts**. If you have this set up, a confirmation window appears.

Figure 2-8: Skype prompts you to verify that you really do want to remove the contact.

3.   Click **Remove**.

Block a Contact

If you want to make sure a person doesn't contact you, you can choose to block them.

To block a person:

1.   Right click on the contact name in the left pane.

2.   Select **Block This Person**. A dialog box appears.

Figure 2-9: The program prompts you to verify if you want to block this person.

3.   If you want to just remove the person from your list and not allow them to call you, check **Remove from your Contact** list.

4.   If you also want to report inappropriate behavior such as unwanted advances or profane language, check the **Report abuse** box.

5.   Click **Block**.

Unblock a Contact

If you made a mistake with blocking a person or later choose to unblock the contact, go to your options window.

To unblock a contact:

1.   Select **Tools, Options**. The Options dialog box opens.

2. Click the **Privacy** button on the left.

3. Click the **Blocked contacts** button.

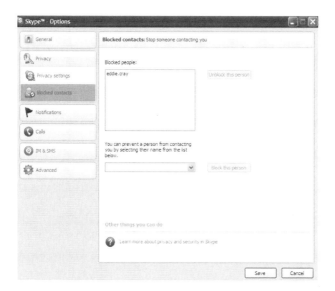

Figure 2-10: The Option window shows you which contacts are blocked.

4. In the **Blocked people** box, click on the person's name and click **Unblock this person**.

5. If you want to block someone in your contact list, select them from the **You can prevent a person from contacting you by selecting their name from the list below** down arrow and click **Block this person**.

6. When finished with the dialog box, click the **Save** button.

See Your Facebook Contacts

Skype allows you to see your Facebook contacts, send messages or emails, and make calls if they have set up email and phone numbers in their Facebook accounts.

To show your Facebook contacts:

1. Click the Facebook icon on the contacts pane, Press **Alt+F2**, or choose **View**, **Facebook Friends**.

2. If you have already set up Facebook to work through Skype, your contacts appear in the left pane. If you have not set up Facebook, click the **Connect to Facebook** button in the left pane.

3. In the right pane, type in your Facebook **Email** address and **Password**.

4. If you want to stay logged in to Facebook each time you go to Skype, click the **Keep me logged in** checkbox.

5. Click the **Log In** button.

Unlink Facebook and Skype

If you want to disconnect Facebook with Skype do the following:

Figure 2-11: When connected with Facebook you can see what is happening with your friends on the Skype Home page.

1.    If indicated, click on the Facebook tab on the left side of the window.

2.   If indicated, click on the **Skype Home** tab on the right side of the window.

3.   Click on the disconnect button and select **Disconnect from Facebook**.

Create a Skype Group

You can create a group of people to call at one time if you have the correct subscription.

To create a Skype group, do the following:

1. Select **Contacts, Create New Group**. On the right side of the window, a dotted box appears.

2. Drag the person from the Contacts pane to the dotted box to the location that says **Drag contact that you want to add here**. Drag additional contacts until you have the contacts you want in that group.

Figure 2-12: Drag from the left pane to the top part of the right window to add people into your group.

3. 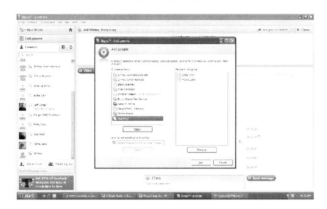 You can also add contacts, by clicking the Plus icon and selecting Add people.

Figure 2-13: The Add people dialog box allows you to add multiple people to your group.

4. Double-click on each name you want added and they appear in your People in this group box.

5. If you want to add someone not in the list, type in the phone number in the **or enter someone's phone number** box and click **Select**.

6. If you accidentally add a name that should not be in the group, double-click to remove the person.

7. Click the **Add** button when finished.

8. Click the **Save group in Contacts** button when complete.

9. You can accept the default name of the members separated by commas or type in a new name and press Enter.

Figure 2-14: Type in the name of your group.

Remove a Contact from a Skype Group

To remove a group from your contacts list:

1. Scroll down to the group name and click on the group name in the left Contacts pane.

2. Do one of the following:

    a. Select **Contacts**, **Remove From Your Contacts**.

    b. Or right-click on the group and select **Remove from your Contacts**.

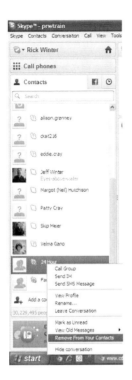

Figure 2-15: Right-click and select Remove From Your Contacts to remove a group or individual.

3. A dialog box may open to ask you to confirm that you want to remove the group from contacts. Click **OK** to confirm the deletion.

Figure 2-16: Skype prompts you to verify if you want to remove the group.

Import a List of Contacts into Skype

You can get contacts from many of your mail programs. You do not have to import from Facebook or Microsoft Outlook. You can choose to have Skype link directly to these programs and turn the link on or off. See the other sections in this chapter for instructions.

To import a list of contacts:

1.   Select **Contacts, Import Contacts**. A window displays with the different email programs listed.

Figure 2-17: Skype allows you to choose from many different email programs.

2. Click on the email program or choose **Other** and select from a list of additional programs.

3. If prompted, enter your user name (often email address) and password for the program.

4. The first screen lists your contacts that have Skype. If you want All users, click on All. If you want a few users, click None and click the box to the left of each person to select or you can unselect users.

5. Click **Add number contacts**.

6. Choose Next. The second screen lists those who are not listed in Skype.

7. If you want all users, click on **All**. If you want a few users, click **None** and click the box to the left of each person to select or you can unselect users.

8. Type in your name and email and edit the default message if necessary.

9. Click **Send email** or **Skip** if you do not want to add any of these contacts.

10. The final screen shows how the contacts appear in your Contacts window.

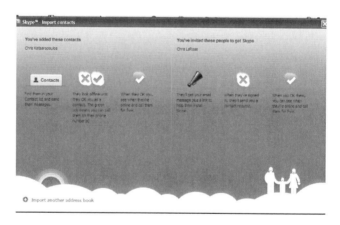

Figure 2-18: Skype shows icons next to contact names when they are online or offline.

11. [Close] If desired, you can click the X close button or **Import another address** book.

Link to Contacts in Microsoft Outlook

You can import Microsoft Outlook contacts into Skype or simply link to Outlook itself to use the contacts in your Contacts List.

To use Microsoft Outlook Contact's list:

1. Select **Contacts, Show Outlook Contacts**.

   Skype lists the contacts in the left pane with an Outlook note below each name.

Figure 2-19: Your contacts appear on the left pane and Outlook displays under their name if they are coming through Outlook.

2. A checkmark appears on this menu item. To unlink to the Outlook contacts, select **Contacts, Show Outlook Contacts** again.

Contact Request

In addition to inviting your own contacts to Skype, there may be times when someone would like to Skype with you.

When someone tries to add you to Skype, a new Contact request bar appears and highlights with a number. The number indicates how many invitations you have.

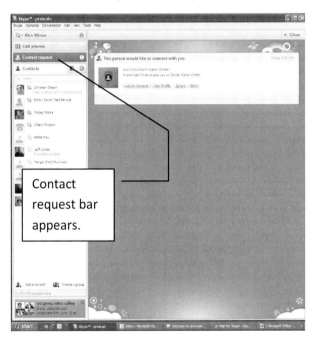

Contact
request bar
appears.

Figure 2-20: The Contact request bar only appears when there is a waiting contact.

To accept or reject a contact request:

1. Click on Contact request bar.

2. If you want to see more about them, click the View Profile button.

3. Do one of the following:

   a. To add them, click the **Add to Contacts** button.

   b. To refuse the contact, click the **Ignore** button.

   c. To not allow them to contact you again, click the **Block** button.

Share Your Contacts

You can also share your list of contacts with another Skype user or request that they share theirs with you.

To share your contacts:

1. Right-click on the contact in the left pane or choose the contact and select **Conversation, Send, Contacts**. The Send contacts window opens.

Figure 2-21: You can choose a number of contacts to share with another person at once.

2. Click each contact you want to share.

3. If you accidentally click on a contact, click again to uncheck the box.

4. When finished, click **Send**. Your window displays the message that you have sent the contacts. Your contact's window displays the Number of contacts received from you.

A Simple Guide to Skype

Figure 2-22: A message appears in your right pane as well as that of the contact you sent the list to.

5.   Click on the down arrow on the **number contacts sent to contact** to see a list of the contacts sent.

Figure 2-23: The down arrow expands to show the list of contacts you sent.

Accept Contacts

After your associate sends you a list of contacts you need to decide whether to accept each contact.

To accept contacts:

1.   Click on the down arrow next to **number contacts received from name.**

Figure 2-24: You can choose which contacts you want to add.

2. For those that you are sure you want to add, click the **Add to Contacts** button for each person. Skype opens the Add a contact dialog box with the person's name and a pre-typed message.

3. If desired, edit the message and click the **Send** request button.

4. Skype may prompt you to add a phone number. Type in the number and click **Add number**.

5. Click the **Close** button to finish the procedure.

6. Repeat steps 2-5 for each contact. If desired, click on the **i** button on the right to see more information about the contact such as where they are from. Click **Add contact** to add to your list or **Close** to skip for now.

Figure 2-25: For each contact you can see their location and website if they have entered the information in their profile.

Backup and Restore Contacts

Once you have a number of contacts entered into Skype, you should periodically back them up in case there is a problem with your program.

To back up contacts:

1. Select **Contacts, Advanced, Backup Contacts to File**.
   The Save dialog box opens

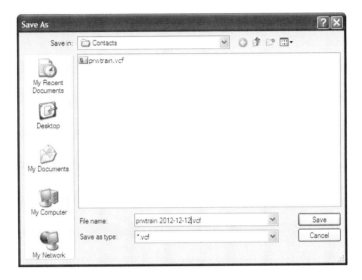

Figure 2-26: Backup your contacts often.

2. Type the name of the backup file in the **File name** box.

3. Click the **Save** button.

To restore your contacts:

1. Select **Contacts, Advanced, Restore Contacts from File**.
   The Open dialog box appears.

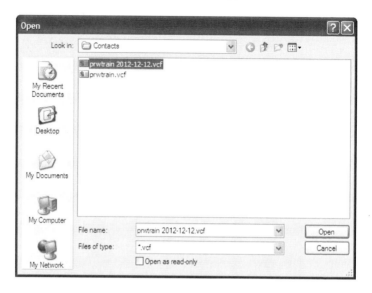

Figure 2-27: If you have backed up your contacts more than once, click on the latest file to restore.

2. Select the name of the backup file.

3. Click **Open**.

Change Sounds

When Skype is dialing the phone, you sign on or off, or any number of other events, Skype plays a sound. You can change the sounds for each event if you desire.

To change a sound:

1. Select **Skype, Profile, Change Sounds**. The Options dialog box appears with the Sounds option selected.

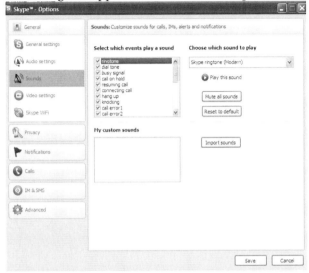

Figure 2-28: Skype shows events and the sound for each event.

2. Click on the event you want to change in the **Select which events play a sound** box.
3. Do one of the following:
    a. Click and select a sound from the **Choose which sound to play** drop-down arrow
    b. Or, click on the **Import sounds** button and navigate to select a sound file.
    c. Or, click on sounds you already have installed in the **My custom sounds** box.

4. After you select a sound, click on the **Play this sound** button to hear what it sounds like.

5. If you don't want any of the sounds to play, click the **Mute all sounds** button or if the sounds are already off and you want to hear them, click the **Enable all sounds** button.

6. Click the **Save** button when finished.

Change Your Password

As with all programs, it's a good idea to change your password every once in a while so people do not impersonate you on the web.

To change your password:

1. Select **Skype, Change Password**. The dialog box opens.

2. Type your current password in the **Enter current password** box. Skype displays asterisks so people standing over your shoulder can't see your password.

3. Type your new password twice in the next two boxes. If your passwords do not match, Skype informs you that you need to type them over.

Figure 2-29: Skype shows that the first password fits the correct pattern, but when it was re-entered the second password did not match the first one.

4. When finished, click the **Apply** button or if you change your mind and do not want to change the password, click **Cancel**.

Set up Privacy Options

You can apply settings in Skype that limit calls, video calls, and instant messages to only those on your contact list or to accept communication from everyone.

To set up privacy:

1. Select **Skype, Privacy**. The Skype Options dialog box opens with Privacy settings selected on the left. Do any of the following:

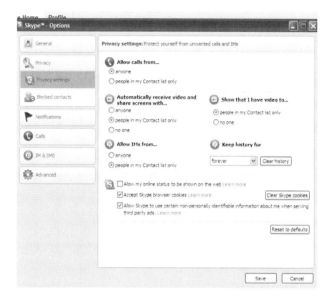

Figure 2-30: Be careful on who you accept calls from.

2. If you only want calls from your contact click Allow calls from ... **people in my Contacts list only** or leave this option on **anyone**.

3. Change the Automatically receive video and share screens with

    a. **no one**, if you do not want to share screens or receive video.

    b. Or, if you want all people to be able to see you and your screen, choose **any one**.

    c.   Alternatively, leave or change this to **people in my Contacts list only**.

4.   You can change the instant messages to Allow IMs from

    a.   **Anyone.**

    b.   Or, **people in my Contacts list only.**

5.   If you want to change the amount of calls recorded to save disk space, click the **Keep history for** drop-down arrow and choose one of the options instead of the default forever.

6.   If you need to remove whom you've called and the associated messages, click **Clear history**.

7.   If you want to create a button for a web page to show you're available, check the **Allow my online status to be shown on the web** and follow the instructions to install the button. If you later want to turn this off, uncheck this box.

8.   Skype allows you to remove the tracking of your progress (who you are, what your preferences are) by clicking the **Clear Skype cookies** button.

9.   Skype gets money by advertising and customizes ads to you based on your browsing history and other factors. If you don't want customized ads, clear the box, **Allow**

Skype to use certain non-personally identifiable information about me when serving third party ads.

10. When finished with all settings, click **Save**.

Voice Messaging

[$] If you want people to leave you voice messages when you don't answer, you can set that up. This either requires a premium subscription or you can pay for each call.

To set up voice messaging:

1. Click **Tools, Options**. The Options dialog box opens.

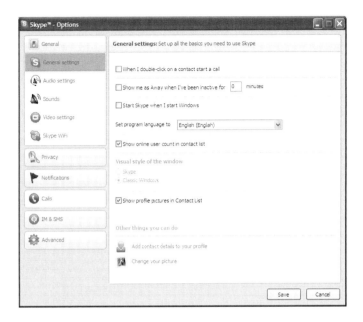

Figure 2-31: The Options dialog box allows you to change many of the program's defaults.

2. Click the **Calls** button on the left. The Calls area opens up to give you more options.

3. Click **Voice messages**.

    a. If you have do not have a subscription, click **Buy Skype voice messaging** or **Get a subscription** to go to the web page to purchase one of these options.

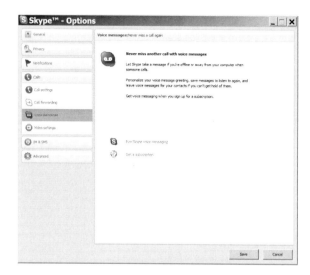

Figure 2-32: This screen is different depending on whether you have a subscription or not.

b. If you do have a subscription, your Window opens to allow you to record your message and set up Voice messaging.

Figure 2-33: When you are ready to set up voice messaging this screen appears after you have paid for the option.

4. Click **Receive unanswered calls as a voice message**.

5. Do one of the following:

    a. [Playback] Click the green **Playback** button to hear the current message.

    b. [Record] Click the red **Record** button to record your message.

    c. [Reset] Click the **Reset to default voicemail greeting** button and confirm by clicking Reset again if asked to return to the default message.

6. To have the voice message played, do any of the following:

   a. In the **Start Recording a voice message if** text box, type in the number of seconds to wait before recording plays.

   b. Click **I reject an incoming call** to turn this recording feature on or off.

   c. Click **I'm already in a call** to turn this recording feature on or off.

7. When finished setting up the recording voicemail features, click **Save**.

Chapter 3

A Tour of Skype

To change your views in Skype:

Figure 3-1: Skype allows you to see your contacts, messages you've sent and activities you've performed.

Skype has many different ways of viewing your contacts and messages. To change the way the screen displays on your computer do any of the following:

To display your list of Skype contacts on the left pane, click the Contact icon, press Alt+1, or choose **View, Contacts**.

To display your Facebook contacts on the left pane, click the Facebook icon, press Alt+3, or choose **View, Facebook Friends**.

To display a list of the contacts you've dealt with in the past few days, click the Recent icon, press Alt+2, or choose **View, Recent**.

Sort Contacts

You can change the way your contacts are arranged so you can see the list alphabetically or to put the online contacts on top.

To sort contacts:

> ➢ Select **Contacts, Sort Contacts by, Name** to see the alphabetical list of all contacts.
> ➢ Select **Contacts, Sort Contacts by, Online Status** to see the list first alphabetically by online contacts and then alphabetically by all those not online.

Limit Visible Contacts

If you have a lot of contacts, there are times you may not want to see the entire list. A checkmark next to the option means this option is turned on. A missing checkmark means the option is turned off.

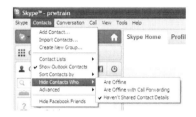

Figure 3-2: This option indicates with the checkmarks that Outlook contacts and those who haven't shared details display.

Use any of the following procedures to show or hide types of contacts:

> ➤ To show or hide people who are on line, select **Contacts, Hide Contacts Who, Are Offline**.

> ➤ To show or hide people who have call forwarding enabled, select **Contacts, Hide Contacts Who, Are Offline with Call Forwarding**.

> ➤ To show or hide people who have not put in details, select **Contacts, Hide Contacts Who, Haven't Shared Contact Details**.

> ➤ To turn on or off the list that shows your Outlook contacts if you have Microsoft Outlook installed, select **Contacts, Show Outlook Contacts**.

> ➤ To turn on the list of Facebook contacts, click the Facebook tab if this is already on or choose **Contacts,**

Show Facebook Friends and select the **Connect to Facebook** button and put in your email and password if necessary.

➢ If your Facebook list is already displaying, **Select Contacts, Hide Facebook Friends** to turn the list off.

Status Symbols

Skype's symbols can help you determine if people are available and the status of messages.

Figure 3-3: In the left pane, Skype shows the status of your contacts.

Online - If someone is online or available for messages or video calls, Skype displays a green checkmark to the left of the person's name in the contact pane.

Phone or mobile number - This is a phone or mobile number and you will need Skype credit or a subscription to call this contact.

Invisible - If someone is a contact and not currently online or has changed their status to invisible, Skype displays an open cloud to the left of the person's name in the contact pane.

Offline - You can change your own status to any of the above options by clicking the down arrow to the left of your name at the top of the screen. In addition to the icons listed above, you can also disconnect by clicking the status down arrow and choosing **Offline**.

Calls Forwarded – Your contact is not available but they have call forwarding or voice mail setup.

Away - If someone has changed their status to Away, an orange cloud appears to the left of the person's name in the contact pane.

Contact request pending – This is a contact that you've invited, but that has not accepted yet.

Conversation – This is a group of contacts.

Blocked – This person has blocked you so you cannot call them.

Do not disturb - If someone does not want to be bothered, a red cloud with a minus appears to the left of the person's name in the contact pane.

Karen H. Winter

If you have one or more messages that you haven't read, Skype displays an orange dot or a circle to the right of the person's name in the contact pane with the number of unread messages.

Skype also displays the number of contacts whose messages you have not reviewed.

Figure 3-4: This contact bar shows that the call lasted for 28 minutes and 14 seconds and displays an end call icon.

Timer - When you are connected to another person, the timer displays the length of the call to the right of the person's name in the contact pane.

End Call - When you are connected to another person, a small red End call button also appears to the right of the timer and person's name in the contact pane. Click this button to hang up the call.

Change Windows Tray Icons

Your taskbar can notify you what events are happening with your contacts.

Figure 3-5: On the right side of your Window in the tray, Skype notifies you when you have a message.

To change which notifications you want to see on your taskbar, do the following:

1. Select **Tools, Options**.

2. Click on the **Notifications** button on the left and choose **Notification settings**.
    The dialog box displays the types of notifications you can receive.

3. If you want to see an example of what the notification looks like on your screen, click the Example button.

Click Show an example. This shows you your taskbar icon and an example message.

Figure 3-6: Use the Options to set your notifications.

4. Click any of the following options to turn the notification setting on or off under the **Display a notification in the Windows tray when someone**…

    a. **comes online**

    b. **goes offline**

    c. **comes online (on Facebook)**

75

d. **goes offline (on Facebook)**

e. **starts an IM with me**

f. **sends me a file**

g. **requests my contact details**

h. **leaves me a voice message**

i. **has a birthday**

j. **sends me contacts**

5. To see messages from your contacts as they send them to you, check the box **sends me a message**.

6. When finished with the changing the settings, click **Save**.

When you have a message from someone, the Windows tray icon changes to the green cloud with an orange dot and a number 1. You can click on this icon to display the message. If you double-click on the icon, it opens up the Skype window and shows you how many messages are from each of the contacts.

Figure 3-7: An orange dot displays on the Recent tab as well as the Window tray icon when you have a message waiting.

 Skype displays a green cloud with a white checkmark indicating you are online.

When you change your status symbol, the change also appears on your Taskbar icon. The changes are the same that appear when you change your Online status: Online, Away, Do Not Disturb, Invisible, and Offline.

Skype Video Toolbar

While you are in a Skype video session, Skype displays a toolbar on the bottom of the screen.

Figure 3-8: Your video session has tools for use during the call.

Figure 3-9: A red slash appears when the camera or microphone is disabled so your contacts cannot see or hear you.

The icons are used for the following:

Show contacts (arrow right) - To turn on the Contacts pane, click the Show contacts button.

Hide contacts (arrow left) - To turn off the Contacts pane, click the Hide contacts button.

Show IM (grey) - To show a pane that allows you to see instant messages, click the Show IM button.

Hide IM (blue) - If the instant message pane is on, click the Hide IM button to turn it back off.

Turn off video - To temporarily turn off the video, click the Turn off video button. On the remote computer the live image is removed and your name and profile picture appears on their screen. You can also select **Call, Video, Stop My Video**

Turn on video - To have the remote person see through your web cam again, click the Turn on video button. You can also select **Call, Video, Turn Your Video On**

Mute your microphone - To temporarily turn off your microphone so the remote person cannot hear you click the Mute your microphone button. You can also select **Call, Mute Microphone**.

Unmute your microphone - To have the remote person hear you, click the Unmute microphone button. You can also select **Call, Unmute Microphone**.

Add send and share - To send a file, picture, or contacts to the remote person, click your Add send, and share button and then choose one of the items on the menu.

End call - To hang up the video and or audio, click the red End call button.

Call quality information - To adjust your video or audio quality, click the call quality information button.

Full screen - To remove the taskbar and Windows title bar, hide the IM and contact panes, and make the image larger, click the Full screen button.

Exit full screen - To return the screen view to display the taskbar, title bar,

Show dial pad - If you are on an audio call only (no video) and need to use the numeric keypad to dial an extension or choose an option, click the Show dial pad button.

Figure 3-10: When you are on an audio (non-video) call, the Hide or Show dial pad button also appears.

Hide dial pad (blue) - If you are on an audio call and need to turn off the dial pad, click the blue Hide dial pad button.

Chapter 4

Text Messages, Phone, and Video Calls

Make a Video Call

If both you and your contact have active web cams and microphones, you can make calls where you are both visible and can hear each other.

To make a video call:

1. Do one of the following:
    a. Click on their name on the contacts pane
    b. Or, begin typing their name in the Search box. If they are one of your contacts, the name appears in the box or in a list.

Figure 4-1: Click on the person's name in the contact pane to display a history of calls and buttons for calling.

2. Select the person and then choose Video call in the right pane. A window opens showing you their profile picture and your current image from your web camera.

Figure 4-2: The person you are calling appears at the top along with your image in the bottom.

3. If they answer, they appear in the camera and your image appears in the upper right hand corner of the screen.
4. If they don't answer, or you want to end the call for any reason, click the End call button.

Add People to an Existing Call

After you start a call, you may want to add additional people. The maximum is 10, but the more people that you add, the slower the connection will be and your system performance may not allow for more than 5.

While in a video call do the following to add people:

1.  Click the + icon on the bottom of the screen.

2. Select **Add People to this Call**. The list of people in your contact list appears.

Figure 4-3: You can see which people are currently online with the green checkmark.

3. Click on each of the people you want to add to the call up to 10. Each person's name appears above the All contacts list.

4. When you've selected all the people, click the **Add to call** button.

Check Files and Messages While on a Video Call

One of the great features of Skype is that you can send files and messages while you are on a call.

To check files or messages:

1. Select **View**.

2. Do one of the following:

    a. Select **SMS Messages**

    b. Select **Instant Messages**

    c. Select **Files Sent and Received**. The left pane opens with one of the lists above.

Figure 4-4: When you click Files Sent and Received, you can see the files that have been shared by the person or people on the call.

3.   Click on one of the bars on the left to view the message. The right pane changes to show you the messages or files.

Click on bar to see file or message.

Double-click to return to view full video images.

Figure 4-5: When you click the bar with the person's name, you can see the messages from that person in the right portion of the screen.

4.   If desired, read the message, click **Save As** to save and then open the file, or **Cancel** sending of the file.

5.   Double-click on the image of the contact you're working with to return to the larger screen to see your video contact(s).

To End Call with One Person

 If you have multiple people on your call, you can leave the call for everyone by clicking the End call button at the bottom of the screen.

Otherwise, to remove one person from the call, do the following:

1. Right click on the screen with the person. A menu appears.

Figure 4-6: Right click on the picture of the person and choose End Call with This Person to finish your call.

2. Select **End Call with This Person**.

Make a Phone Call

[$] You can call another person on Skype without video. You can make the call to a land line or cell phone if you have a subscription or pay the added charges (unless the phone is a toll free number). If the other person has Skype, you can call their computer for free and talk if they have a microphone.

To make a phone call:

1. Do one of the following:
   a. Click on their name on the contacts pane
   b. Or, begin typing their name in the Search box. If they are one of your contacts, the name appears in the box or in a list.

Figure 4-7: When you start typing the name "M" in this message, this shows people with an M at anywhere in their first or last name.

2. Click on the person in the Contacts pane.

3. Do one of the following:
   a. Click the **Call** button if there is only one phone or you want the default phone number.
   b. Click on the **Call arrow** button and choose the phone you wish to dial.
   c. Click **Add phone number** if the number is not in the list and type in the new phone number.

Figure 4-8: The call down drop down option allows you to call the person through Skype, their mobile, office, or add another phone number is this example.

4. If they answer, they appear in the camera and your image appears in the upper right hand corner of the screen.
5. If they don't answer or you want to end the call for any reason, click the End call button.

Tip: If you want to call a business that is not a toll free number, check for free gas, movie show times or the check the weather, you can do this even without a subscription or Skype credit. Call BING411 (800-BING411 or 800-2464) and use your microphone to provide ask for the lookup information.

Dial a Phone Number

[$] You can call a phone number that is not a contact. This is an extra charge unless you have a Skype subscription or it is a toll free number.

To dial a phone number through your computer:

1. Click the **Call phones** bar.

2. If you need to change the country, click the down arrow and select a country.

3. Click on the numbers in the numeric keypad or type the numbers with your keypad.

4. Click the **green Call** button.

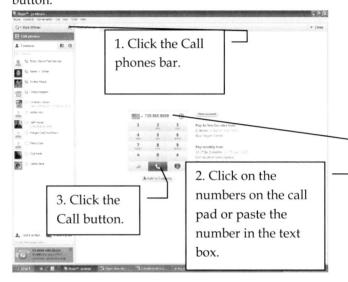

1. Click the Call phones bar.

2. Click on the numbers on the call pad or paste the number in the text box.

3. Click the Call button.

Figure 4-9: You can use the call pad to call a number not in your list of contacts.

To copy a phone number from anywhere to the dial pad:

1. Highlight the phone number in whatever program has this listed.

2. Press Ctrl+C, right-click the highlighted area and select **Copy**, or choose **Edit, Copy**.

3. Go to the Skype window.

4. Click the **Call phones** bar.

5. Click in the area that says **Enter number**.

6. Press Ctrl+V, right-click and select **Paste**.

7. If you need to change the country, click the down arrow and select a country.

8. Click the **green Call** button.

Note: You must have paid for a Skype subscription or have Skype credit if you are calling a cell phone or a land line.

Send an Instant Message

Skype can send instant messages to those that are on Facebook, have Skype, or have the option on their Internet enabled cell phones.

To send an Instant Message:

1. Do one of the following:

    a. Click on a name on the contacts pane.

    b. Or, begin typing their name in the Search box. If they are one of your contacts, the name appears in the box or in a list.

    c. Right-click on a name and select **Send IM**.

2. On the bottom half of the right screen, type in the message.

Figure 4-10: The person's name is selected and the message appears in the middle of the right pane before you send it.

3. If desired, click the emoticon symbol and click on the symbol you want to include in your message.

Figure 4-11: You can associate different kind of faces or other icons with a message.

4. Click **Send message** when done. Depending on their cell phone or if they are in Skype, they will receive the message.

5. As they type you will see a pencil on the screen.

A Simple Guide to Skype

Figure 4-12: When you are IMing each other – both you and your contact messages appear in the right pane.

Send an Instant Message to a Group

You can also send an IM to a group. The contacts within the group will get the message when they login to Skype.

1. Click on the Group name in the Contacts pane.

Figure 4-13: You can call or send messages to a group of people.

2. In the right pane, type your message. If you want to send to their phones for an extra charge, click the **SMS** checkbox.

3. If desired, add an emoticon.

4. Click the **Send message** button.

Send an SMS Message

[$] Skype can send SMS messages cell phones. However, you will need a subscription or Skype credit to make the call. Some phones have both SMS and IM capabilities so you may want to try IM first since it is currently free.

To send an SMS Message:

1. Do one of the following:

    a. Click on a name on the contacts pane.

    b. Or, begin typing their name in the Search box. If they are one of your contacts, the name appears in the box or in a list.

    c. Right-click on a name and select **Send SMS Message**.

2. On the bottom half of the right screen, type in the message. If SMS is not checked because you started with option a or b above, click the **SMS** checkbox.

Figure 4-14: Type your message under the yellow bar.

3. Click **Send message** when done. The next time they have their phone on, they will receive the message.

Figure 4-15: Click the blue Send message button to send the message.

Send a File

You can send files to your Skype contacts.

If you want to give them the option of receiving a file when they logon to Skype:

1.   Do one of the following:

     a.   Click on a name on the contacts pane, click the + button and choose **Send File**.

    b.   Or, begin typing their name in the Search box. If they are one of your contacts, the name appears in the box or in a list, click the + button and choose **Send File**.

    c.   Right-click on a name and select **Send File**.

2.   In the Send File dialog box, navigate to the file and click **Open**.

Figure 4-16: Click the Look in and change the location of the file or choose the Up One Level icon to change where you find your file.

3.   The file appears in your window with a Waiting message.

Figure 4-17: The file name with "Waiting" appears in your right pane.

4. Depending on what the contact does, you will receive one of two messages on your right pane.

Figure 4-18: After a person receives the file, the message says, "File sent." If they refuse the file, the message says, "Sending Cancelled."

a. If they accept the file, you will see File sent.

b. If they click Cancel, you will see Sending cancelled.

Send a File While on a Call

You can also send a file while you are on a call. The icons on the bottom of the screen give you options.

To send a file while you are on a call, do the following:

Click the plus icon on the bottom of the screen or select **Conversation, Send, File**. The Send dialog box opens.

Figure 4-19: Select the file you wish to send.

1. Navigate to the file and click **Open**.

Receiving a File

If you have received a file while you are not on a call with a contact, the person's name shows an orange dot next to their name and the Skype icon displays a number in the Windows tray.

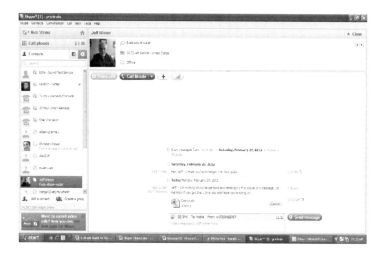

Figure 4-20: There is an orange dot to the right of Karen H. Winter's name.

To receive the file, do the following:

1. Click on the contact's name in the left pane. The Skype window shows that a file is waiting.

Figure 4-21: The right pane shows the file and a Save as and Cancel buttons.

2. Do one of the following:

    a. Click the **Save as** button if you know the file is safe.

    b. If the file is something suspicious or you don't want it, click **Cancel** and confirm that you want to not receive the file.

3. If you choose Save as, the Accept file box may open unless you've disabled this option. Choose **OK**.

Figure 4-22: This dialog box warns you that there may be viruses in the file. Make sure you know the sender.

4. In the Save dialog box, choose the location where you want to save the file and click **Save**.

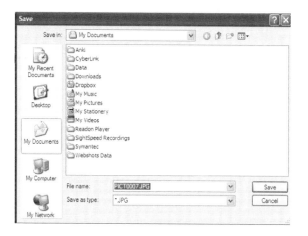

Figure 4-23: This PICT0007.JPG file will save in My Documents folder.

5. Skype shows you that the file is saved and you can open the file or the folder. Do one of the following:

Figure 4-24: The PICT0007.JPG file is a picture.

a. Click **Open file** to display the file.

b. Click **Show in folder** to display the folder where the file was saved.

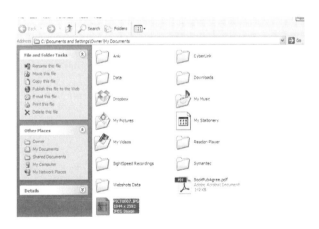

Figure 4-25: This window shows that the PICT0007.JPG is saved in this folder.

Receiving a File During a Video Call

While you are on a video call, you can receive a file in a couple of different ways.

To receive a file while on a video call:

1. The toolbar displays an orange dot next to the Show IM button.

Figure 4-26: An orange dot appears on the IM button indicating that there is a waiting file.

2. Click the **Show IM** button.

Figure 4-27: You can click Save as to keep the file or Cancel to reject the file.

3. If you want to reject the file, click the **Cancel** button and confirm that you want to cancel by selecting **OK**.

4. If you want to accept the file, click on the **Save as** button.
    If you haven't turned off the feature, Skype will warn
    you about viruses and suggest you only accept files from
    people you know.

**Figure 4-28: Skype allows you to turn off this warning by
checking the Do not ask me again button before you click
OK.**

5. Click **OK** to accept the file. The Save dialog box opens.

Figure 4-29: You can change the location by clicking the Save in down arrow or double-clicking on any of the folders in the screen.

6. Navigate to where you want to save the file, type in a new name if desired, and click **Save**. After you receive the file, Skype provides you two options:

Figure 4-30: The Show in folder is in blue next to the file name.

    a. Click **Open File** to display the file.

    b. Click **Show in folder** to show a list of all files in the folder where you saved the document.

Sharing Your Screen During a Video Call

In addition to seeing your face, you can also show the person what you are working on during a video call. One use of this is to open a Word document and take notes during the phone call. Another could be to discuss files you are working on together.

If you want the person you're calling to also see your screen, do the following:

During the video call, click the + button on the bottom if the screen or select Call.

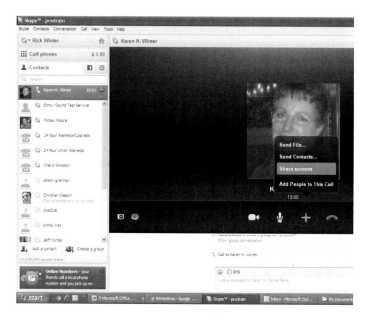

Figure 4-31: Choose the Share screens option to allow the person to see your screen too.

1. Select **Share screens**.

2. A small Start sharing window appears. Do one of the following:

Figure 4-32: You can see a small version of their screen before you click Start.

> a. Click the down arrow on the bottom left corner and choose **Share desktop** to display everything (this is the default).
>
> b. Click **Share window** to display a specific window. Choose the window you wish to share.

3. Click **Start** to begin the sharing.

4. When you are finished click the **Stop sharing** button at the top of your screen.

Figure 4-33: An icon to Stop sharing appears when you are in share screen mode.

5. ![End call button] When you are completely done with the call, click the End call button.

Answering a Call

Not only will you be sending calls, but you will be receiving them as well. When someone is calling you, there will be a sound (depending on your settings) and an incoming screen.

To answer the call:

1. When someone is calling you, a popup window appears with his or her profile picture and three buttons:

Figure 4-34: A small window opens with a picture of the person and name if they have included this in their profile.

2. Do one of the following:

   a. Click **Answer** for voice only.

   b. Click **Answer with video** for both voice and video.

c.   Click **Decline** if you cannot answer the call right now. If they have voice mail set up, you can record a message.

Transfer a Call

In addition to answering a call, you can also transfer the call to one or more of your contacts. If you transfer the number to a landline or mobile phone, additional charges may apply if you don't already have a subscription.

To transfer a call:

1.   When someone is calling you, a popup window appears with his or her profile picture and three buttons and a transfer button.

Figure 4-35: The button after Decline is transfer call.

2.   Do one of the following:

a.   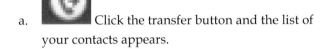 Click the transfer button and the list of your contacts appears.

b. Click **Call, Transfer Call**. You can also choose this option if you are already in an existing phone or video call.

3. Do one of the following:

a. Check the contact(s) you want to transfer the call,

Figure 4-36: Your available contacts appear in the list.

b. Or, click the **Enter another phone number** button and enter a different number.

4. If desired **Enter a message for the person you are transferring the call to** in the box.

5. Click the **Transfer** button.

Viewing History

You can see the messages between you and a contact for the last day, last 7 days, or last 30 days.

To look at the history of calls and messages:

1. Click on the person's name in the left Contacts pane.

2. Click on **Yesterday**, **Last 7 Days**, or **Last 30 Days**. The window changes showing the messages that have been sent back and forth.

Figure 4-37: The right pane shows the message sent between you and your contact.

Getting Out of Skype

Skype takes up a lot of memory, but if you use it a lot, you may want it running in the background to receive calls.

To get out of Skype do one of the following:

If you want to have the program running in the background to allow calls to come in, select **Skype, Close**. To reopen the program, you can double-click on the Windows tray icon.

➢ To turn off Skype and not be available, click **Skype, Sign Off**. Skype returns to the login screen. Click the **Close** (X) button to get out of the window.

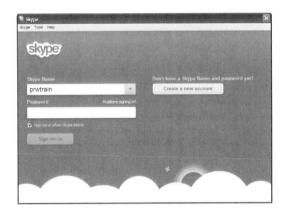

Figure 4-38: The X Close button on the top right of the screen allows you to close this window.

➤ To remove Skype completely from memory, right-click on the Skype taskbar icon and choose **Quit**. You are warned that you cannot receive instant messages or calls.

Chapter 5

Troubleshooting and Notes

This chapter explains a few additional things you should be aware of when you are using Skype.

Emergency Calls

Skype does not do allow for emergency calls (911 in the US and Canada, 112 in Europe, 999 in the United Kingdom and many other countries, 111 in New Zealand, 000 in Australia). For this reason, is it recommended that you maintain your land line or mobile phone to make emergency calls. However, one option is to call your emergency service dispatch office and ask if there is an alternative number you can program into Skype. A problem with this is that emergency services may not be able to pinpoint where you are, especially if you have a laptop and move from place to place.

Skype Etiquette

Skype is like other communities in that there are certain norms of behavior that are expected. When your face is visible, this may help a bit compared to voice or email only conversations to allow people to see your humor, but the screen may not show all of your nonverbal cues that would be visible in a person-to-person live conversation. Skype has some suggested rules of etiquette on how we treat each other available at

http://www.skype.com/intl/en-us/legal/terms/etiquette/.
The main point is to be aware of what the person or people
you're communicating with and how they may perceive
messages or what they might find offensive.

**Figure 5-1: When you are not talking with someone in person,
there is a higher change that your message could be
misinterpreted. Please follow online etiquette suggestions.**

Getting Skype Help

You can get Skype help in different ways from within Skype and
from the Skype Internet home page.

1. Do one of the following. In both cases, the Help window
   opens.

a.   While in Skype, click **Help, Get Help**.

b.   While in an Internet browser, type
www.skype.com, press Enter and click on
Support.

Figure 5-2: Help displays on the Internet for Skype.

2.   If you want to see answers to common questions, click
on any of the Top FAQs or How-to guides.

3.   If you have a special question not listed on the screen,
type in the Search box and click Search.

4.   If you want see what the latest Skype questions are or
get help from others using Skype, click Go to the
Support Network. Scroll down to see the most recently
Frequently Asked questions, Account questions,
questions on specific operating systems or devices

(Windows, Mac, Mobile), questions about products, and so forth.

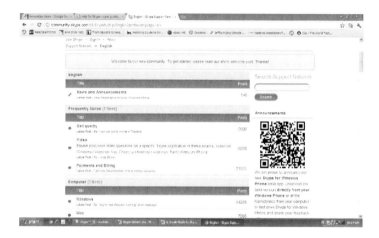

Figure 5-3: The Support Network is a live area where people are currently asking questions.

Skype Heartbeat

You can see if there are any issues world- or country-wide affecting a number of Skype users at once.

To check for issues that would affect many people at once:

1.   Do one of the following:

a. From an Internet browser, type
   heartbeat.skype.com and press Enter.

b. From within Skype click **Help**, **Heartbeat**.

Figure 5-4: This window shows that your online number, SMS, sign in, accounts, payments are all working correctly.

2. Scroll down to see issues that have happened on recent days.

A Simple Guide to Skype

DATE DUE

6/10/14	

MAY '13